Hans Christian Andersen

Oxford University Press, Great Clarendon Street, Oxford OX2 6DP

Oxford   New York
Athens   Auckland   Bangkok   Bogotá   Bombay
Buenos Aires   Calcutta   Cape Town   Dar es Salaam
Delhi   Florence   Hong Kong   Istanbul   Karachi
Kuala Lumpur   Madras   Madrid   Melbourne
Mexico City   Nairobi   Paris   Singapore
Taipei   Tokyo   Toronto   Warsaw

and associated companies in
Berlin   Ibadan

Oxford is a trade mark of Oxford University Press

Text © Andrew Langley 1997
Illustrations © Oxford University Press 1997

A CIP catalogue record for this book is available from the British Library

ISBN 0-19-910437-9 (hardback)
0-19-910443-3 (paperback)
0-19-918654-5 (Branch Library Pack B)
1 3 5 7 9 10 8 6 4 2

Printed in Dubai by Oriental Press

Hans Christian Andersen

THE DREAMER OF FAIRY TALES

ANDREW LANGLEY

Illustrated by Tony Morris

OXFORD UNIVERSITY PRESS

When he was a boy, Hans Christian Andersen loved to make up stories. He would sit for hours in the tiny yard at home, with his mother's apron over his head to keep out the sun. He invented plays for his dolls, and even made a toy theatre for them!

Hans was born in 1805 in Odense, a town in Denmark. His father was a shoemaker, and his mother a washerwoman. They were so poor that they had only one room. But being poor did not bother Hans. He was a dreamer, and found magic all around him.

Hans never played with other boys. They were rough, and made fun of his lanky legs and his strange stories. He liked to be alone, reading books or playing with his doll theatre. When he was seven, Hans saw his first real play, at the town theatre. He was entranced. There and then he decided to become a famous actor.

At the age of fourteen, Hans climbed aboard a coach clutching a bundle of clothes. Soon he was rattling out of Odense. He was on his way to Copenhagen, Denmark's capital city. He was bursting with hope and excitement. His life in the theatre was about to begin.

But it seemed that no-one wanted poor Hans. The director of Copenhagen's theatre told him he was too thin and clumsy to be an actor. Others thought he was mad. They laughed at this strange boy in his wide hat, frilly shirt and enormous boots.

Now Hans had no money. In despair, he knocked at the door of a well-known musician. The musician was having a party, but he invited Hans in.

The guests watched as Hans danced, sang and recited poems. Then they clapped and cheered. "He will go far!" said one. They gave Hans money, and the musician promised him free singing lessons. Perhaps his dream would come true after all.

Hans worked hard. He went to his singing lessons, and even learned to dance. But it was no good. Everyone told him he would never be graceful or handsome enough to be a success on the stage.

Now Hans had another idea. He was good at making up stories. Perhaps he could become a famous writer! In a rush, he wrote a play – then another – and another. But nobody liked them.

The trouble was that Hans had learned very little at school. His writing was messy and his spelling was dreadful. But now came the luckiest moment of his life. He met Jonas Collin, a director in the theatre. Collin took pity on him, and paid for him to go to a grammar school.

So at the age of seventeen, Hans started proper schooling. He hated it! He was much older than the other pupils, and too big to sit comfortably at his desk. Worse still was the headmaster, Dr Meisling. He was a fierce and bad-tempered man, who shouted at Hans, calling him stupid and lazy. For the rest of his life, Hans had nightmares about the terrible Dr Meisling.

It was a happy day for Hans when he left school and began to study at Copenhagen University. Jonas Collin still looked after him. Hans went to Collin's home every day, and became close friends with his children. For the first time in his life, he was part of a big happy family.

Hans spent every spare moment writing. And, at last, he was a success. His first book sold well. Then one of his plays was performed at the city's biggest theatre. He began work on a long story.

3y the summer of 1829, Hans had earned enough money o take a holiday. He made a tour of Denmark. One day, ıe called at a friend's house, where he met a pretty girl ıamed Riborg Voigt. Hans fell madly in love with her. Ie and Riborg went on walks and boating trips. Hans vrote poems for her. But the love affair was a short one. Riborg decided to marry someone else, and Hans was ıeart-broken.

Over the next three years, Hans became a well-known writer. His poems, plays and stories sold all over Denmark. Now he wanted to see more of the world. The Danish king granted him enough money for a long trip abroad.

So Hans set out on his next great adventure. First he went to Germany, then to France. Paris, the capital of France, seemed to be a wonderland, with its grand buildings and milling crowds. Here, Hans met other famous writers and composers.

He travelled on to Italy. This was even more wonderful! Hans loved Rome so much that he stayed there for four months, looking at the churches and ancient ruins. He told a friend that the city "has opened my eyes to beauty".

There was plenty of fun as well. During Rome's great carnival, crowds filled the streets, dancing, singing and throwing confetti at each other.

Back in Copenhagen, Hans settled down to a cosy life in his little apartment. His poems and stories had made him famous all over Europe. But so far all his books had been for grown-ups. Now he was ready to try something quite different.

Each morning he sat in front of a crackling fire, wearing his dressing gown and brightly-coloured slippers. The tea kettle hissed gently on the table. Hans day-dreamed, just as he had done when he was a child.

All sorts of things came into his head – strange stories, and funny people he had met or seen. Hans began to write down the stories, putting the funny people into them. They grew into fairy tales, the first he ever wrote.

Eagerly, Hans completed four tales. Among them were "The Tinder Box" and "The Princess and the Pea".

They were published in 1835, in a volume called *Fairy Tales for Children*. This was the turning point in Hans's life.

Girls and boys loved Hans's tales. They thought they were the most wonderful stories they had ever read. Wherever Hans went, children came to give him flowers, or toys, or even kisses.

Many of Hans's tales were about magical things that could never really happen. There was Thumbelina, the girl so tiny that she slept in a walnut shell. There was the Snow Queen, who lived in a palace made of snow and freezing winds. And there was the Little Mermaid, who loved a Prince so much that she became a human.

Other tales were about everyday life. It was quite easy to believe in the poor Ugly Duckling, who grew up to be a beautiful swan. And then there was the stupid Emperor, who was tricked into buying a set of invisible clothes, and went about naked!

Over the next fifteen years, Hans wrote many more fairy tales. Some grown-ups sneered at them. They said that the stories were too cruel and violent for children. They also said that the stories were badly written!

Hans was a lonely man. Like his own Ugly Duckling, he was different from other people. Although he fell in love many times, he never married or had a family of his own. But every day he would visit friends and talk to their children.

Often, the talk would turn into a story. Hans could make up tales out of nothing, or make something new from an old fairy story. And he was never dull. The children sat entranced as his tales grew and grew, full of jokes and magic.

While he talked, Hans would fold a piece of paper. Then he would take out his scissors and snip away carefully. When he unfolded the paper, there would be wonderful shapes, all joined together – castles or angels or goblins or swans. People were amazed that someone who looked so clumsy could make something so clever and fine.

In 1840, Hans set out on his travels once more. This time he went much further than before. From Italy, h took a steamship to Greece. Then he went on eastwards to Constantinople, the famous city which stoo between Europe and Asia. There he crossed over into Asi Minor (today this is part of Turkey).

Asia Minor was still a wild land, and few Europeans had visited it. Hans saw many strange sights. Most amazing of all were the dancing dervishes, or holy men, of Pera. Hans watched in delight as they whirled round and round, their long skirts standing out like upturned funnels.

Soon it was time to go home. Hans chose the most dangerous route – up the great River Danube. Many travellers had been killed in this wild region, but Hans was not scared. He was much too excited by the beautiful scenery!

Hans had dreamed as a boy of kings and queens, princes and princesses. Many of his stories were about them. Now that he was famous, he met these people in real life. It was like a fairy tale come true

In the summer of 1844, Hans went to stay with the King and Queen of Denmark. He dined with them every day, and read some of his stories aloud. Next, he travelled on to Germany, where he stayed with a duke, then a prince, then a bishop and then another king!

Hans loved being with these grand people, who had such dazzling clothes and beautiful houses. He did his best to dress up smartly. At one banquet he wore a three-cornered hat, and a sword at his waist. But his new boots were so tight that he nearly fainted.

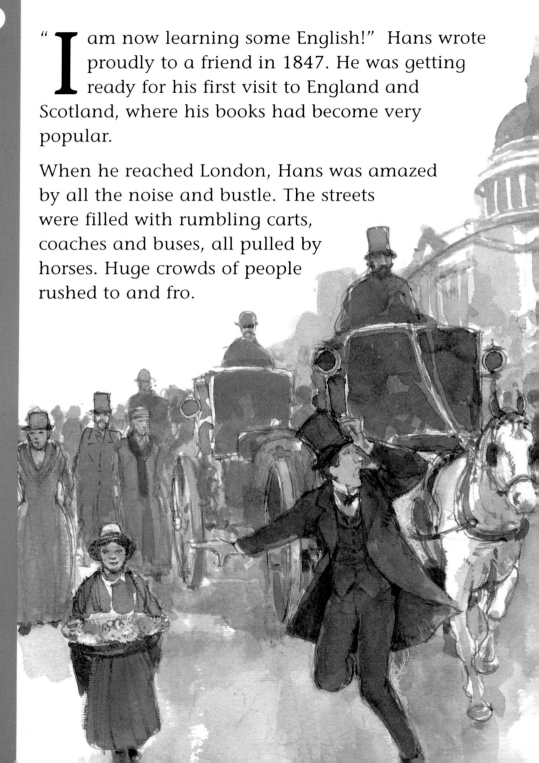

"I am now learning some English!" Hans wrote proudly to a friend in 1847. He was getting ready for his first visit to England and Scotland, where his books had become very popular.

When he reached London, Hans was amazed by all the noise and bustle. The streets were filled with rumbling carts, coaches and buses, all pulled by horses. Huge crowds of people rushed to and fro.

The visit was a rush, too. Hans was invited to parties and dinners and dances almost every day. Everybody wanted to meet him. But Hans himself wanted to meet one person above all – the great English novelist, Charles Dickens.

One evening, Hans was at a grand dinner party. Into the room bustled a short, lively man. It was Dickens. Hans ran to shake his hand, and the two famous writers greeted each other warmly. They soon became firm friends.

Hans still lived alone, but he had many friends. He would visit a different friend for dinner each day. Hans also had thousands of friends that he had never seen. These were the children, from all over the world, who loved his fairy tales. One little girl kept a book of his stories under her pillow. She thought Hans Andersen must be an angel, because he could write so well!

Then one day she was lucky enough to meet him. With his big nose, long arms and lanky figure, he did not look much like an angel. All the same, he was a magical person to be with.

Hans and the girl often went for walks. He might find something in the grass – a dead flower, or an insect. Picking it up, he would tell a long story, all about its life and adventures. He seemed to be able to make a story out of anything.

One day a friend challenged Hans to write a story about a needle. He thought that it would be impossible, because needles are not very interesting. But Hans did write a wonderful little story called "The Needle", and put it in his next book.

When he was a little boy, Hans had met a strange old woman. He had thought she was a witch. She had said that one day the town of Odense would be lit up in his honour.

The old woman was right. Sixty years later, the people of Odense held a special ceremony in honour of Hans Christian Andersen. A procession marched through the streets, carrying banners and blazing torches.

Hans watched from a window of the town hall. He heard the townsfolk singing songs and cheering, just for him. He should have been very happy – but instead he was in agony. He had toothache!

Hans was growing old, and suffering from all kinds of illness. Some of these were real, but others were imaginary. His greatest fear was that, when he was asleep, people might think he was dead. So he put a notice by his bed, saying "I am not really dead".

In his long life, Hans visited many countries, but he never went to the USA. He was angry with the American publishers, because they sold thousands of his books and never paid him any money for them. He complained that he had not received a single dollar from America.

One day, Hans had a letter from a little American girl. Inside it was a dollar bill. The girl explained that she wanted to pay Hans what the publishers owed. Hundreds of other letters came, all with dollar bills inside. Hans was upset that so many children thought he was poor!

Hans died in August 1875. A statue of him can still be seen in Copenhagen. And there is a statue of his Little Mermaid in the nearby harbour. Hans would be thrilled to know that children all over the world still love his fairy tales.

Important dates in Hans Christian Andersen's life

1805 Born in Odense, Denmark.
1819 Leaves home and goes to find his fortune in Copenhagen.
1822 Goes to the grammar school of Dr Meisling. His first book, called *Youthful Attempts*, is published.
1833 Makes his first long trip abroad, to Germany, France and Italy.
1835 His first book of fairy tales is published.

1840 Another journey abroad, as far as Greece and Turkey.
1847 First visit to England and Scotland; meets Charles Dickens.
1867 Given the freedom of Odense in a special ceremony.
1870 Writes his last book, a story called *Lucky Peer*.
1875 His seventieth birthday is celebrated all over Denmark; he dies in Copenhagen.

Index